Mendel Nun

THE SEA OF GALILEE AND ITS FISHERMEN IN THE NEW TESTAMENT

Published by Kinnereth Sailing Co.
Kibbutz Ein Gev

THE SEA OF GALILEE AND ITS FISHERMEN IN THE NEW TESTAMENT

Introduction

Old and New: Contrast of Sources

The Sea of Galilee and the profession of fishing are mentioned in both the Old and New Testaments. However, the two sources differ considerably in the historical value and implications of their descriptions.

The Old Testament mentions the Sea of Galilee by its oldest biblical name "Yam Kinneret" (Sea of Kinneret) four times, in connection with the borders of the Promised Land and the allotment of the twelve tribes. In Hebrew and Aramaic, "Yam" can mean both Sea and Lake.

The name "Sea of Galilee" appears for the first time in the New Testament, which also gives several other names: Sea of Tiberias, Sea or Lake of Gennesar or Gennesaret. It is mentioned many times and its attributes provide the background for daily life.

The descriptions of the fishermen's craft also differ widely in the two sources. In the Old Testament little is said about fishing, although the main fishing implements are named, and we will deal with several of them.
But we find no reference to any personality who is a fisherman, or to any event directly concerned with fishing. All that is said in the Old Testament regarding fishing is in the form of parables and allegories. It

Egyptian fishermen, 25th century B.C.

Etruscan fishing boat, 5th century B.C.

appears that most of the prophets were familiar with the fisherman's occupation, as we shall see. At the same time, the influence of Sumerian and Accadian literature is apparent to a greater or lesser extent, in most of their writings, where the tools of fishing and hunting are used as allegories.

The Gospels describe fishing in a different way, for obvious reasons: the Sea of Galilee was the scene of most of Jesus' ministry, and fishermen and sailors were his earliest disciples and followers. It was to them that he first preached, standing on the shore of the lake. As his audience grew, he began to preach from fishing boats, and his disciples kept ready for him a small boat for this purpose. For longer trips Jesus sailed in the boats of fishermen, to teach in the towns and villages of the region.

This is why the New Testament contains vignettes, parables, and descriptions of the fishermen's life. But even so, we cannot expect to find full detailed professional accounts, and for several reasons.

The problem of Gospel chronology and language has long been argued by scholars. The earliest sources about Jesus are accounts and oral traditions written or passed on in Hebrew and Aramaic by Jesus' followers after his death. We can only assume that among these texts, those that deal with fishing were authentic for their day. It is now generally believed that the decades after the year 60 were the period during which the Gospels as we know them were composed and appeared in Greek.

These writers, some of whom were already distant from Jesus' life on the lakeshore, did not intend to write historical texts, but rather stories with a religious message to be read at early Christian gatherings. Therefore, they adapted the texts and reshaped them according to their theological purposes. This process accounts for the difficulties in understanding the fishing narratives and natural phenomena described in the Gospels.

4

The commentators and translators of the Old Testament and of the Gospels have one thing in common: they had difficulty with the descriptions of the fishing because they had no practical experience with the craft. Consequently, mistakes continue to appear in dictionaries and encyclopaedias.

Furthermore, the writers of the Gospels relied largely on the Septuagint, and it appears that not all the seventy were familiar with the Greek names for the various nets. Thus, there are inconsistencies in translations for these nets. From the Septuagint, this confusion was carried over into the translations of the Gospels into all other languages.

Those who translated the Gospels from Greek into European languages "solved" the problem by using the generic word "net" for all kinds of nets, as in the Greek "dictyon". This is also true of modern translators of the Gospels into Hebrew.

However, to identify the fishing methods and nets mentioned in the Gospels, we shall concentrate on the details of the operations as actually carried out. Let us, at the start, state that fishing methods on the lake did not change from the time of the Second Temple up to modern times, that is, up to 1955, when the techniques used on the lake were revolutionised. In 1948, the Arab fishermen, who had preserved the ancient tradition, left the area, and with them the old methods faded away. In 1960's cotton thread was replaced by synthetic invisible lines, which made possible daytime fishing with the same nets. The fish population changed as well. Indigenous species declined, and new species were introduced. The fishermen used motor driven boats made of fibreglass and electronic fish detectors. Enormous innovations thus changed the face of the Sea of Galilee.

It is impossible to explain and to comment on the fishing episodes of the Gospels without a familiarity with the main original species of fish and the methods by which they were caught in ancient times.

Sumerian fisherman,
27th century B.C.

Egyptian fisherman,
25th century B.C.

The Fish Population of the Lake

The indigenous population consists of 18 species, 10 of which are commercially inportant, and most of which are endemic to the lake or to the Jordan water system. The remainder are small inshore species, insignificant in number and quality. According to tradition, the edible fish of the Sea of Galilee are classified locally into three main groups, 1) Musht (which includes the St Peter's Fish), 2) Biny (Barbels), 3) Sardines.

1. **Musht**. "Musht" means "comb" in Arabic, because the five species of this group have a long dorsal fin, which looks like a comb. The biggest, the most common and the most important of these is the Tilapia Galilea, which can reach a length of 40 cm and may weigh 1,5 kilogram. The body has a silvery colour, which gave it the Arabic nickname "Musht Abiad", meaning White Musht. The flat shape makes it suitable for frying. The skeleton consists of an easily detachable backbone and relatively few small bones, and thus it is easy to eat. We will refer to it simply as musht.

With the cooling of the waters of the lake as winter starts, the musht congregate and move in shoals, especially toward the northern part of the lake. When the water warms up in the spring, they disperse and we find pairs of these fish living together for as long as one to two months - a phenomenon unusual for fish. After a prolonged courtship, the pair digs a hollow in the soft bottom of the lake near the shore or in a lagoon, and deposit the eggs. After fertilization, the parents take the eggs into

Tilapia galilea, "Musht" - St. Peter's fish

6

A Musht "couple" during spawning ceremony

their mouths for two or three weeks, until they hatch. Even after the young are hatched, the parents keep watch over the young fry for a few days; this is the source of its modern Hebrew name "Amnun" - "am" in Hebrew meaning nurse, and "nun" meaning fish. This concern of the family's welfare is typical of all members of this widespread tropical family. The musht is the only large fish which moves in shoals, a point that is important for our subject, as will become clear.

Musht parent with young

7

2. Biny group (Barbels). This group consists of three species of the Carp family (Cyprinideae), which is widely represented in this region. The characteristic of this family are the barbs at the corners of the mouth; from these comes the Semitic name "Biny", which means hair (in the Babylonian Talmud the fish are called "Binita"). Of the three, only two have economic importance.

A. Barbus longiceps, the Long Headed Barbel (Kerseen in Arabic) is a handsome trout-like fish with a narrow silvery body and pointed head. It can reach a length of 80 cm, and a weight of 6 or 7 kg. It feeds on molluscs and snails at the lake bottom, and on small fish especially sardines. In the past, as spring approached, the Kerseen migrated to the southern outlet of the Lake and to the Jordan river to lay their eggs and return; later, the young fry also returned to the lake. However, since 1932 this outlet has been closed by a dam, and an iron mesh prevents the fish from making their traditional migration.

B. Barbus Canis has larger scales. In Arabic it is called "Kishri" meaning "scaley". It is smaller than the Kerseen, with a larger belly. It reaches 50 cm in length and its weight may reach 3 to 4 kilos. It is a

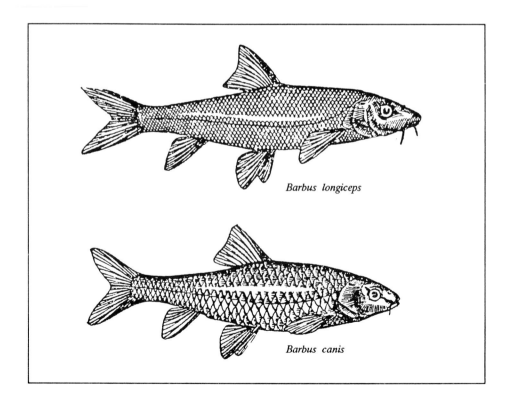

Barbus longiceps

Barbus canis

predatory fish, feeding on small fry and is therefore always found near schools of sardines, which are caught together with this fish. This barbel reproduces during the summer along the shore.

Both barbels are well fleshed and popular as the fish dish for the Sabbath and feasts. This is why they have always had an important place in the Land of Israel. The Talmud describes how Tiberias fishermen brought seven barbels as a gift to the Patriarch Yehuda haNasi during his stay in the city.

The Hafafi (Varicorhinus damascinus) also belongs to this group. The elongated body resembles the Long Headed Barbel, but is much smaller. It is yellow, the scales are small, and the belly is soft. It feeds on decaying matter found in mud, which affects the flavour; therefore its value is not great. Because it was originated in rivers north of this region, this fish shares a trait with the salmon: in winter, when the streams are full and cold, it swims and even jumps upstream to their source to lay its eggs. Another trait is that on these migrations it interbreeds with the Long Headed Barbel; the offspring are called by the Arabs "bastards" but they are still considered members of the Biny group.

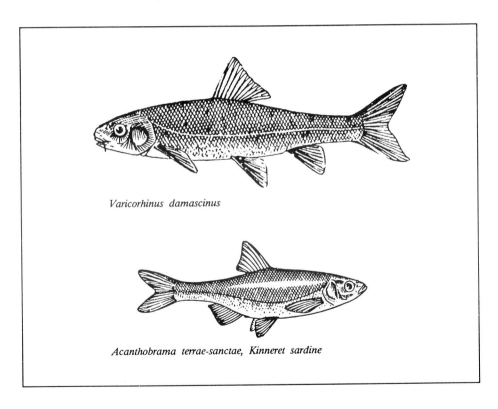

Varicorhinus damascinus

Acanthobrama terrae-sanctae, Kinneret sardine

3. The Kinneret Sardine (Acanthobrama terrae sanctae), in Arabic "Sardine Tabariya", is the smallest of the commercial fish and endemic to the lake. Nevertheless, it has great economic importance because of its extensive distribution, and constitutes more than half of the yearly catch. It resembles the saltwater sardine, an like it can be found in enormous schools. At the height of the fishing season, tens of tons of sardines are caught every night. This is why they were conserved by pickling, already in antiquity. The center of this industry was the town of Magdala, hence its name Migdal Nunia, Migdal of the Fish. In the Talmud, the sardine - both the saltwater varieties from the Mediterranean and the sweetwater sardines from the Kinneret, as well as this fish in its preserved form, were known as "Tarit". It was an important part of daily food throughout the country, and especially for those who lived near the lake.

Catfish (Clarias lazera), Arabic Barbut, Hebrew Sfamnun, meaning Mustached Fish. This is an unusual fish, the sole representative of its African family. It is the largest of the original fish in the lake, growing to a length of 1,25 meters, and may weigh up to 10 kilogram. Because it has no scales, it may not be eaten by Jews, which reduces its economic importance. Josephus Flavius refers to the catfish by its Greek name of "Korakinos", meaning Water Raven; he notes that it is found in the Nile. In his opinion, this fact supports the popular belief that there was an underground connection between the Nile and the lake, and that it emerged from below the ground at the largest spring at Tabgha.

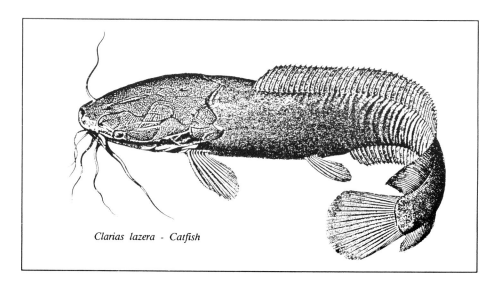

Clarias lazera - Catfish

Introduced species

Silver carp (Hypophtalmichthys molitix), originally a native of China. Does not reproduce in the lake. Its fingerlings are hatched in local laboratories. Today, the largest fish in the lake, reaching 50 kilos.

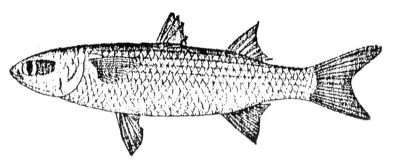

Grey mullets (Mugil cephalus, Mugil capito). Fingerlings are brought from streams flowing into the Mediterranean, because these species too do not reproduce in the lake. Today, the most commercially important fish in the lake.

Common carp (Cyprinus carpio). Although this carp reproduces in the lake and thousands of fingerlings are added every year, it has nevertheless not become commercially important.

The Boats and the Catch

In the 1940's the annual catch of fish from the Kinneret amounted to 400-500 tons. In the eighties, it reached 1,800 to 2,000 tons, including the newly introduced species of grey mullets and silver carp - an impressive catch for a lake whose surface is only 170 square kilometers. Today there are about 65 small fishing boats, four large vessels (purse seiners) and about 150 fishermen in the peak season. In the off season, only half of this fleet is active. Most of the fishermen are Tiberians; the remainer are from Kibbutz Ein Gev and Kibbutz Ginnosar, and the village of Migdal.

Tabgha - The Fishermen's Suburb of Capernaum

The name Tabgha is a corruption of the Greek name Heptapegon, meaning Seven Springs. And indeed, two kilometers west of Capernaum we find a group of springs varying in volume, temperature and salinity. Josephus Flavius refers to the largest as the Well of Capernaum, thus pointing to the connection between the two. It is known today as Ein Nur, and is enclosed within an ancient octagonal stone tank.

Mosaic from 6th century church, Transjordan

The fishing harbour of Tiberias, 1975

The harbour of Ein Gev, home port of the Kinneret Sailing Company

13

The springs of Tabgha have great economic importance. In the winter, the warm water draws schools of warmth-loving musht, tropical in origin, to the vicinity. The waters of the springs were once used to operate several flour mills. The Capernaum fishermen stayed in this area during winter and early spring, making Tabgha an important industrial suburb of Capernaum. A small harbour which served the millers and fishermen was found in the nineteen seventies.

When Jesus began his ministry, he left his native Nazareth and came down to the lake. Capernaum became "his own city", and he lived with the family of Peter, the fisherman. It was winter and the family were all working in Tabgha. Here, on the shore, Jesus began to preach, and found his first followers and disciples among the fishermen. Most of the events in the Gospels connected with fishing therefore took place at Tabgha. According to Christian tradition, this is also the place where Jesus met with his disciples after the resurrection.

Tabgha and its warm springs, the best fishing ground for St Peter's fish.
Left and right, ruins of ancient flour mills.

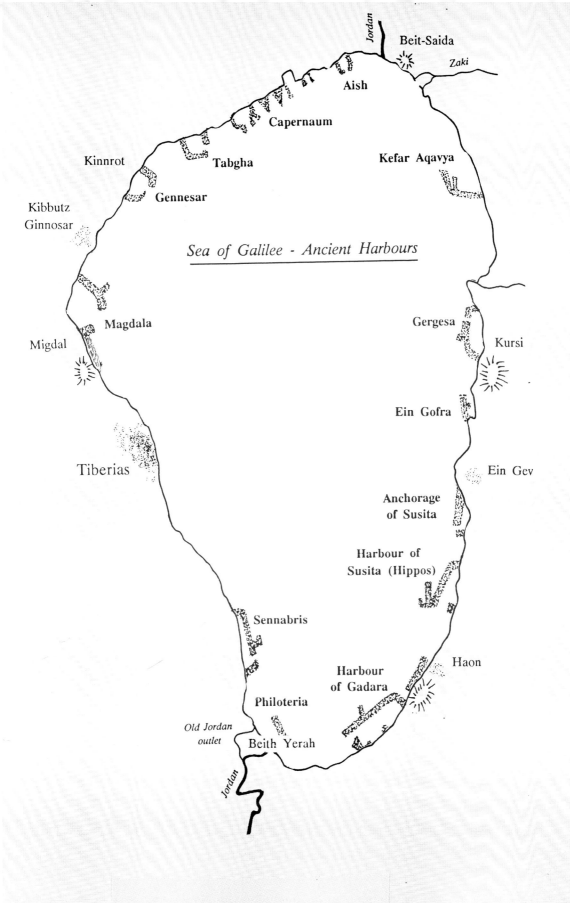

Sea of Galilee - Ancient Harbours

Jordan

Beit-Saida

Zaki

Aish

Capernaum

Kefar Aqavya

Kinnrot

Tabgha

Gennesar

Kibbutz
Ginnosar

Gergesa

Kursi

Magdala

Migdal

Ein Gofra

Ein Gev

Tiberias

Anchorage
of Susita

Harbour of
Susita (Hippos)

Sennabris

Haon

Harbour
of Gadara

Philoteria

Old Jordan
outlet

Beith Yerah

Jordan

The Seine (Dragnet)

The Seine is the oldest type of net, and was once the most important fishing method on the Lake. In the Old Testament and the Talmud it is called "Herem" (Arabic Jarf; Greek Sagene, from which, obviously, our word is derived).

The dragnet is made of netting shaped like a long wall, 250 to 300 meters long, 3 to 4 meters high at its "wings" and 8 meters high at the centre. The foot-rope is weighted with sinkers, and the head-rope has cork floats. The dragnet is spread a hundred meters or more from the shore and parallel to it, and hauled toward the shore with towing lines consisting of sections of ropes tied together. These are attached to each end, and hauled by a team of 16 men for large nets, or a smaller team for smaller nets.

From Egyptian grave paintings since the third millenum B.C., and from other sources, we may assume that this fishing method was widely used in the ancient countries of the east.

The following description is the writer's recollection of his personal experiences as a fisherman in the nineteen forties and fifties:

In the early morning the crew assembles to arrange the heavy net on the "table" of the stern of the boat and hurriedly sails off to "catch" a good

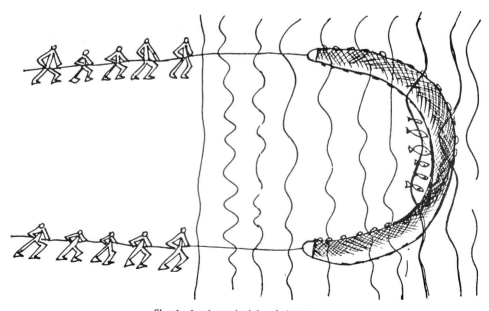

Sketch showing principle of dragnet

16

Dragging the seine: Egyptian fishermen, 16th century B.C. (above)
Ein Gev fishermen, 1938 (below)

fishing area. This is why, as we shall see, the Talmud refers to this net in the description of "detaining" the boat. When we arrive at the fishing grounds and the boat touches shore, half the crew alight and take the first rope. The boat sails out with the trailing line until it reaches the end of the line. The boat then turns and sails parallel to the shore until the net is "spread". The boat then turns back to the shore trailing the second set of ropes. On reaching the shore, the remaining half of the crew alights and takes the end of the other towing line, leaving the boat "detained" on the shore.

The whole team now harness themselves to the ropes and pull the net to the shore. The sinkers have dragged the net to the bottom, the floats have lifted the head-rope, and the net now forms a rectangular wall that advances to the shore with its lower edge at the bottom of the lake. The two groups of fishermen climb from the water up the beach, moving also toward each other. The seine method utilises the nature of fish to dive to the bottom and to try to escape toward the deep water when they are in danger. Thus the fish in the space surrounded by the dragnet are caught.

As the net comes near the shore, the skipper takes the boat and when necessary dives from it to lift the foot-rope over possible obstacles such as stones protruding from the bottom. With the ropes slung across their shoulders or around their hips, the fishermen make their way up the beach. The one who is farthest up the shore goes back to the water, takes up his harness again, and joins those in the line. This continues until all the ropes are out of the water. Then the fishermen sit down in the shallow water and haul the net until it is piled up on the shore. The central, higher section of the net, called the bunt, is made of thicker thread and finer meshing. At the end of the operation the fish are concentrated in the bunt ("Zuto" in the Talmud) and a good catch may bring in hundreds of kilos.

Setting the seine: Ein Gev fishermen, 1938

The whole operation takes an hour or more, depending on the number of seine ropes tied together - in other words, the distance from shore at which the net was spread and began to move. After this operation is completed and the fish sorted, the net again arranged on the stern, and the ropes coiled and placed in the boat, the work starts over again at another location, and may be repeated as often as eight times during a day's fishing. In summer a wooden box with holes is trailed behind the boat to keep the catch alive. Because of its weight and the relatively large crew, the dragnet method requires a large boat - usually about 8 meters long and 2.5 meters wide. It is of interest that these are the dimensions of the ancient boat from the time of Jesus discovered in the mud of the lake in 1986, near Magdala. Arab fishermen of the lake call this kind of boat "Arabiya".

The income from the catch was divided according to the ancient fishing tradition of "shares" (Arabic "housa"). Forty percent went to the owner of the boat and net, the remainder to the crew. The skipper ("raiss" in Arabic) received two shares together with certain other benefits from the owners. His second in command and menders of the net received one and a half parts, and those who hauled the net - one share each. During the British Mandate, eight such dragnet crews "swept" the coastline and caught about half of the annual catch of the big fish. In the mid-fifties this method was replaced by more modern techniques.

Arab fishermen dragging the seine, near Bethsaida, 1930

Tank of plastered stone at ancient harbour of Gergesa
for storing live fish caught by seine

Lead sinkers for seine net found in the harbour of Gergesa

An ancient tradition preserved in the Talmud,* tells of the exclusive fishing rights given by Joshua bin Nun to the Tribe of Naphtali, entitling them to "set seines" (herem) around the entire shoreline. To enable them to exercise this right, a strip of land at the southern tip of the lake belonging to the Tribe of Gad, was added to the lot of Naphtali. In width it was designed as equal to "the full seine rope", which came to about 40 or 50 meters when ropes were thick and heavy.

The seine or dragnet ("herem") is mentioned in the Old Testament nine times, or more than any other methods. In Habakkuk 1:14-15 we find a lively description of dragnet fishing which is generally translated inaccurately. Correctly, as translated by the author, the passage should read: "And makest men as the fishes of the sea, as the creeping things, that have no ruler over them? They take up all of them with the angle,

---

* b.B. Kam 81a,81b. T.B. Kam VIII 17.

they drag them in their seine and gather them in their trapnet; therefore they rejoice and are glad." In the following verse Habakkuk mentions the "fat portion" of the owner of the seine.

The prophet Ezekiel refers three times to the "place of the spreading of seines": 26:5, 26:14, 47:10. Seines laid out to dry flat on the ground are a recurring picture for fishing villages. The Talmud calls the fishermen of Tiberias after their main equipment, the "seine men of Tiberias" (Haramei Teverya).

"Place of spreading of seines"
Fishermen mending the seine at the inlet of the Jordan, 1925

The Parable of the Seine

In the Greek version of the Gospel according to Matthew, the dragnet is called by its Greek name "sagene", when Jesus uses it to explain allegoricaly his teaching of the Kingdom of Heaven. "Again, the kingdom of heaven is like a net which was thrown into the sea and gathered fish of every kind; when it was full, men drew it ashore and sat down, and sorted the good into vessels but threw away the bad" (Matt. 13:47-48).*

This fits exactly the function of the dragnet. It is cast into the sea, then dragged to the shore; in the process all kinds of fish are caught, which the fishermen sitting on the shore sort out. The "bad" ones refer to the scaleless catfish, forbidden by Jewish law and not even offered for sale.

There is only one inaccuracy in this description: the words "when it was full", as though there were some period of waiting for the net to fill. The basic feature of dragnet fishing is to start hauling immediately as soon as it is spread. If this is not done, the fish would escape and the whole operation would fail. We may assume that this slight inaccuracy is due to the wish to emphasise the theological message of the parable.

---

* This and all following quotations are from the Revised Standard Version of the New Testament, 1952.

Ancient mooring stone (left) and stone anchors, found around the lake

The Cast-Net

The cast-net (Hebrew Kela, Arabic Shabakeh) is circular, measuring from 6 to 8 meters in diameter, with bars of lead attached to the edge, and used by a single fisherman. He arranges it on his right arm, and standing in shallow water or in a boat, throws it forcefully out on the water, where it lands like a parachute and sinks to the bottom. Like the seine, the cast-net is an ancient device. Complete cast-nets were found in Egyptian tombs dating to the second millenium B.C. Two kinds of cast-nets were used on the lake, one for large fish and the other for sardines. The sardine cast-net was thrown from a boat; it had a small mesh and a system of cords for retrieving.

The cast-net for big fish has a larger mesh and heavier sinkers, to prevent the fish from escaping before the net reaches the bottom. The fisherman using this net must approach his prey silently and without casting a shadow.

There are two ways of retrieving the catch. The fisherman may dive down to the net, pull the fish one by one through the meshing or out of the net and put them in a pouch. Or he may dive and gather all the sinkers, lift the edges carefuly over the stones, and take the net up into the boat with the catch inside. When cast from shallow water, and especially if the catch is heavy, the net is dragged to the shore.

Throwing the cast-net from a boat

Roman oil lamp from Alexandria, decorated with picture of cast-net fishermen

Since the middle of the fifties, cast-nets are no longer used in commercial fishing. The Old Testament does not mention the cast-net as such, though there may be a reference to it in the expression, "to spread a net over...", as in Ezekiel 32:3; "Thus saith the Lord God; I will therefore spread out my net over thee with a company of many people; and they shall bring thee up in my seine". (In the King James version, the word net appears for seine).

The ancient tradition preserved in the Talmud, mentioned in the previous section, tells of the exclusive right given to the Tribe of Naphtali by Joshua Bin Nun: "to set the herem and spread the kela". The "herem" was generally identified with the seine. But confusion remains concerning the kela, which in Hebrew has several meanings, among them sling, curtain, sail, rope and braid; as a verb it also means throw, cast, hurl. This is why most of the modern commentators of the Talmud - who were not themselves fishermen - missed the exact meaning of the kela as a fishing net and understood by it "to set sail". Thus the implication becomes that the exclusive right of Naphtali was to set sail in the lake. For this reason, there is rarely a dictionary translation for "kela" as net. A similiar confusion in translation occurred in another part of the same passage. The commentators did not understand that "detaining the boat" is actually a part of the operation of "spreading the seine" and not, as is often written, to anchor a boat.*

---

* This is the source of the error that the exclusive fishing rights to the Tribe of Naphtali were to set sail and anchor a boat. The real meaning is the right to set the seine and spread the cast-net.

Cast-net fishermen at the inlet of the Jordan, 1930

Sardine fishermen using cast-nets, c.1925

*Sixth century mosaic from church in Hirbet Bet-Loya (Negev)
showing fishermen brothers with musht and cast-net (Peter and Andrew?)
(Courtesy of Israel dept. of Antiquities and Museums)*

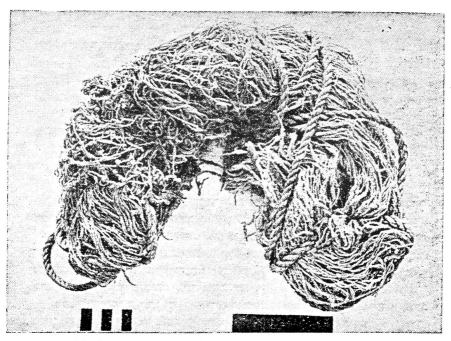

*Section of linen net found in cave near Ein Gedi, from the time
of Bar Kochba, 2nd century C.E. It closely resembles a modern net.
On view at Israel Museum, Jerusalem.*

The Hebrew name kela reflects the action of casting the net. In this it is similiar to the Greek "Amphiblestron", which, like "kela" contains the root "ballo" meaning throw. The full translation of Amphiblestron is "to throw around", and the thrower of the cast net is a frequent theme in Roman-Byzantine mosaics.

The Cast-Net in the Gospels

The cast-net is mentioned in the Greek versions of Mark and Matthew, in its exact full Greek name. As the two versions are almost identical, we give the following quotation from Mark: "And passing along by the Sea of Galilee, he saw Simon and Andrew the brother of Simon casting a net in the sea; for they were fishermen. And Jesus said to them, "Follow me and I will make you become fishers of men. And immediately they left their nets and followed him" (Mark 1:16-18).

From the text, it appears that the brothers had nothing to leave but their nets. But according to Luke 5:3, Simon had a boat and other fishing gear, while Jonah's family must have been wealthy as they owned a house in Capernaum. Peter puts it most clearly: "Lo, we have left our homes and followed you." (Luke 18:28). It appears that the story as written in Mark, with the brothers leaving their nets as though these were all their worldly goods, was intended primarily to underline a religious message.

Throwing the cast-net from shallow waters, 19th century drawing

27

The Trammel Net

Arabic, and used in Hebrew: Ambaten (M'batten)

The trammel net is the only one used in ancient times that is dominant on the lake today. Its Arabic name indicates its special construction. Unlike other nets which have only one "wall", this is a compound net consisting of three layers held together by a single corked head rope and a single leaded foot rope. The two external walls are identical, and 1.8 meters high. The German name "Spiegelnetz" (mirror net) derives from this construction. These outer walls have large meshes measuring 12.5 cm from knot to knot. The middle layer is made up of a fine, normally meshed net, 3.5 to 4.5 cm from knot to knot, but is higher than the outer walls and hangs loosely between them, and can slip in an out between the outer nets, This resembles a lining and explains the Arabic name M'batten, meaning lining or lined. Even today, small 5 to 6 meter long fishing boats on the lake are called M'batten boats, after the main net they use.

The trammel net has another special characteristic. It is always used as at least five units attached to each other. Each unit is 35 meters long, and is called in Arabic "Joz", meaning pair, and reminding us again of the "mirror" concept.

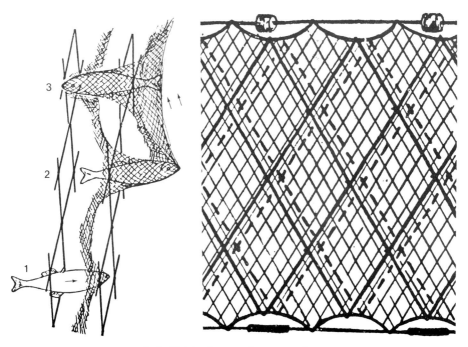

Left: Sketch of trammel net operation.
Right: Sketch of three-walled construction of trammel net

Tabgha a hundred years ago. Trammel nets hang on wall of an ancient flour-mill. At right, ancient cistern enclosing a mineral spring

Trammel net fishermen at Tabgha today. Background: Church and Rock of the Primacy, the traditional site from which Jesus directed the fishermen in the miraculous draught (John 21:6). At right: ancient flour mill and harbour

Tiberias lakefront, 1928

Needle used to make and repair netting, bronze, 14 cm,
first century, found at Magdala

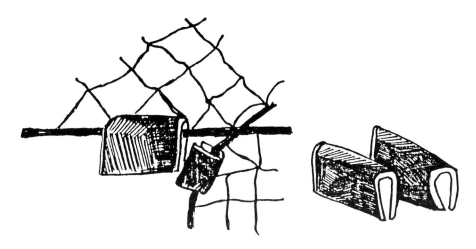

Left: Portion of net with lead sinkers found in a 14th century B.C.
Egyptian tomb. Right: Ancient lead sinkers found along the shore
near Magdala, actual size

There was a type of trammel net used for fishing musht, and another for barbels; they differed in thickness of thread and size of meshes. In the Roman period, fishing nets were made of linen thread. A linen net from the time of the Bar Kochva rebellion was found in a cave near Ein Gedi. Cotton, imported from India and even cultivated in Palestine, replaced flax and was used in these nets until it was replaced in turn by synthetic fibres.

Here is this writer's recollection of a scene with fishermen working with a trammel net boat:

The fishermen meet on shore in the early evening, mending their nets and tying them together while arranging them on the stern. Sailing or rowing to the fishing grounds, they quietly lower the net into the water so that it forms a wide curve, with the open side parallel to the shore. The leaded foot rope pulls the net to the floor of the lake and the floating line keeps the net upright. In deep water, the net can be spread in

31

different shapes, even in spiral form. After the net has settled, it stands like a wall on the lake floor. Gourds, and later empty tins, are used as floats, tied to the two ends of the net and serving as signs in the dark marking the position of the net.

Now the boat enters the area between the net and the shore. The fishermen begin to make noise and turbulence by splashing with their oars and stamping on the bottom of the boat to terrify the fish (a performance which frequently irritated residents living on the shore). The frightened fish dive to the bottom, and in their flight toward deep water, find themselves facing the net. Now the fish passed easily through the large mesh of the first layer, but immediately comes to the narrow meshing of the middle layer. Pushing against it, he takes it through the third wall. Trying to retreat, he finds himself hopelessly entangled in a kind of net bag. Now the net is hauled out and the fish disentangled by hand, one by one. The net is prepared for the next operation, and the boat moves on.

This process of extracting the wriggling fish from the fine meshing of the bag without letting it escape, and without cutting the fisherman's hand, is a real art. This explains why fishermen so often have swollen hands during the musht season.

Usually the net is lowered and hauled up ten to fifteen times during a night's work, but it is also possible to leave it in the water for several hours, or even for a whole night. A good night's catch may bring about 50 to 100 kilos (approximately 100 to 200 pounds) of fish. When a trammel net is lowered in the middle of a school during the musht season, hundred of kilos may be caught. Veteran fishermen even speak of memorable single hauls of as much as half a ton.

When the catch is large, the fish are not extracted one by one; instead the net is hauled into the boat like a bundle with the fish entangled inside, and the fishermen will spend considerable time disentangling them.

When the night work is finished, the sections of the net are separated, and each part is washed and rinsed in the lake so it will be free of silt. Then it is hung up to dry on poles or on a wall. It is important to emphasize that the process of washing a net in the morning is specific to the trammel net.

Fishing with the trammel net was usually done at night, when the fish could not see the threads of the net; during the day, they could avoid it. During the musht season, the trammel net is also effective at twilight if the net is spread in spiral form in deep water.

It is interesting to note that the trammel net had an ancestor, namely,

*Trammel nets being dried after the night's fishing, Ein Gev,
during tower-and-stockade period, 1937-41 (Photo Naphtali)*

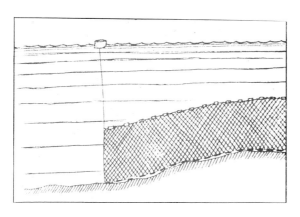
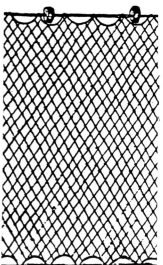

Sketch of gill-net

the gill-net, which consists of one wall made of fine netting. It is set in the evening and retrieved in the morning. Fish swimming innocently in the darkness are caught in the mesh by the head, behind the gill cover. This net was known in the Sea of Galilee early in this century, but was rarely used for barbels. However, with the introduction of strong modern netting, it has became popular for sardine fishing as well.

The Bible refers to these two entangling nets as "Metzuda", or "Matzod" (meaning "trap" in Hebrew). The writer of the Book of Ecclesiastes uses these nets to express his pessimistic view of the fate of mankind. "For man also knoweth not his time, as the fishes that are taken (entangled, in the Hebrew text) in an evil net..." (Ecc. 9:12).

In Job, these nets symbolize a situation from which there is no escape: "Know now that God hath overthrown me, and hath compassed me with his (entangling) net... He hath fenced up my way that I cannot pass, and He hath set darkness in my paths" (Job 19:6-8).

The Veranda Net
Arabic, Sharak koussayb, Sharak; same name used in Hebrew.
In order to catch the schools of wily leaping musht (St Peter's Fish) by day, the early fishermen of the Lake adopted a method common in the Mediterranean which is still in use for catching the grey mullets, a fish with the same characteristics of moving in schools and leaping. The veranda net (known in the Mediterranean as tihweek) is a combination of the trammel

net with other nets used in the lake. The point of this combination is to keep the trammel net afloat horizontally with transverse reed canes (koussayb in Arabic). The circle of the floating canes is thought to resemble the rays of the sun. This is why the term Sharak ("east" in Arabic) is used locally.

It was used as follows. As soon as a school of musht was detected, usually with the help of an observer on shore, the school was surrounded

Above: Contemporary Egyptians fishing for grey mullets with veranda nets
Below: The veranda net with its floating canes is set around an enclosed
school of musht by a fisherman from Kibbutz Ginnosar (1955)

The Anchorage of Tabgha, where Jesus' disciples moored their fishing boats

either by a dragnet without towing lines, or by a high trammel net. The school was thus enclosed, as though in a barrel extending from the lake bottom to the surface. As soon as the school is so contained, a second boat comes to spread the horizontal trammel net around the floating head rope of the circle. The musht which try to escape out of the "barrel" by jumping over its rim, land on and are entangled in the floating trammel net. In order to startle the fish and make them jump, more trammel nets are spread out in a spiral in the inner circle. Finally, those brave and cautious individual fish that had not jumped were now caught by cast-nets thrown into the center of the "barrel". These nets, as we know, must be retrieved by divers.

A word of comfort to the non-fishing reader: our description of how these various nets function is very detailed and technical. But, as will be seen, an understanding of all these operations is essential for a real comprehension of the Biblical texts.

The Trammel Net in the Gospels

Only the Gospels, of all our historical sources, preserve clear indications of work with the trammel net.

"And going on a little farther, he saw James the son of Zeb'edee, and John his brother, who were in their boat mending the nets. And immediately he called them; and they left their father Zeb'edee in the boat with the hired servants, and followed him." (Mark 1:19-20).

Matthew's version is almost identical, but he does not mention hired servants: "And going on from there he saw two other brothers, James the son of Zeb'edee and John his brother, in the boat with Zeb'edee their father, mending their nets, and he called them. Immediately they left the boat and their father, and followed him." (Matt. 4:21-22).

We already know that Jesus met his first disciples on the shore of Tabgha during the musht season. The mention of "nets" in the plural points with certainty to the trammel net, which consists of five separate parts.

Trammel net boat, 19th century drawing

Two further points: 1. Fishermen working their trammel nets at night mend them by day; but when work is pressing, as during the season at Tabgha, urgent mending is done in the boats. 2. A trammel net boat, which is 5 to 6 meters long, was until recently manned by a crew of four; today only two are needed. Zebedee's family, with a father and two sons working together, were likely to have a larger boat that could handle a seine and could also be used for transport during the off season. Such a boat would have a larger crew, consisting of the family and hired men.

The Miraculous Draught
Now that we are familiar with the trammel net, we will have no difficulty in understanding the story of the miraculous catch as told in the Gospel of Luke. "While the people pressed upon him to hear the word of God, he was standing by the lake of Gennes'aret. And he saw two boats by the lake; but the fishermen had gone out of them and were washing their nets. Getting into one of the boats, which was Simon's, he asked him to put out a little from the land. And he sat down and taught the people from the boat. And when he had ceased speaking, he said to Simon, 'Put out into the deep and let down your nets for a catch.' And Simon answered, 'Master, we have toiled all night and took nothing! But at your word I will let down the nets.' And when they had done this, they enclosed a great shoal of fish; and as their nets were breaking, they beckoned to their partners in the other boat to come and help them. And they came and filled both the boats, so that they began to sink" (Luke 5:1-7).

It is not difficult to interpret this story. The two boats belonging to the two pairs of brothers were working in partnership that night; because of the limited area of the grounds at Tabgha, this was exactly how fishing was organized there until very recently. And as usual, in the morning the nets were washed and rinsed, which was done only for the trammel nets. The second clue confirming that these were trammel nets is found in the use of the plural form, "nets".

While Jesus was preaching from the boat he saw a school of musht nearing the shore, as often happens during the morning hours of the winter. Following Jesus' command, Simon's boat immediately takes off, the nets which had been already washed are re-arranged and lowered at the spot indicated by Jesus. The catch was enormously successful! In fact, the nets were so full that they began to tear as they were hauled into the boat; furthermore, there was no room for the overflowing nets on the one boat.

38

Jesus preaching at the Sea of Galilee, by Gustave Doré
"He entered into one of the ships, which was Simon's..."

"The Miraculous Draught of Fishes", painting by Raphael (1483-1520).
"Depart from me; for I am a sinful man, O Lord"

Simon's crew call to their partners' boat for assistance. The boat swiftly arrives and takes some sections of the nets on board.

Finally, let us recall how Luke included Jesus' call to the two pairs of brothers: "But when Simon Peter saw it, he fell down at Jesus' knees, saying, 'Depart from me, for I am a sinful man, O Lord.' For he was astonished, and all that were with him, at the catch of fish which they had taken; and so also were James and John, sons of Zeb'edee, who were partners with Simon. And Jesus said unto Simon, 'Do not be afraid; henceforth you will be catching men.' And when they had brought their boats to land, they left everything and followed him." (Luke 5:8-11).

This is a true fisherman's story, even if perhaps a trifle exaggerated, and greatly resembles the recollections of many veteran Kinneret fishermen who even today still recall extraordinary catches of musht with a single haul of a trammel. This is an experience that cannot be repeated today: the musht population has been decimated by the extreme efficiency of modern fishing.

The Miraculous Draught According to John

"After this Jesus revealed himself again to the disciples by the Sea of Tibe'ri-as; and he revealed himself in this way. Simon Peter, Thomas called the Twin, and Nathan'a-el of Cana in Galilee, the sons of Zeb'edee, and two others of his disciples were together. Simon Peter said to them, 'I am going fishing.' They said to him, 'We will go with you.' They went out and got into the boat; but that night they caught nothing.

"Just as day was breaking, Jesus stood on the beach; yet the disciples did not know that it was Jesus. Jesus said to them, 'Children, have you any fish (anything to eat)?' They answered him, 'No.' He said to them, 'Cast the net on the right side of the boat, and you will find some.' So they cast it, and now they were not able to haul it in, for the quantity of fish. That disciple whom Jesus loved said to Peter, 'It is the Lord!' When Simon Peter heard that it was the Lord, he put on his clothes, for he was stripped for work, and sprang into the sea. But the other disciples came in a (small) boat, dragging the net full of fish, for they were not far from the land, but about a hundred yards off.

"When they got out on land, they saw a charcoal fire there, with fish lying on it, and bread." (John 21:1-9)

The story of the Miraculous Draught as narrated by John closely resembles Luke's version, and both apparently originate in the same source. But there are also differences. The most basic is John's characteristic approach, which emphasizes the philosophical-religious message rather than historical or technical details. This is why John's narrative appears vague with respect to the fisherman's viewpoint.

In spite of the differences in details, the two are similiar in essence: in both, after an unsuccessful night's fishing, Jesus directs his disciples to the enormous school of fish, and after the Miraculous Draught he confers on them the fateful mission. Another similarity is that in John's narrative too, the trammel net is identified by its characteristics - the casting of the net at dawn at a distance from the shore, and hauling the net with the catch into the boat.

But there is also a new element in John's fishing story. The help of an observer from the shore and Peter's dive into the water, first naked and then wearing a loincloth, imply that the trammel net was used here by the veranda method. As we know, in this method two boats work together and in the final stage the fisherman dives to retrieve the cast-net from the bottom. The distance "about a hundred yards off" the shore also fits the picture of the veranda method.

One question remains: how many boats participated in the Miraculous

Sketch showing veranda fishermen casting and retrieving cast-nets
"Jesus stood on the shore; ...Then Jesus saith unto them,...
Cast the net on the right side of the ship, and ye shall find"

Cast-net fishermen; Roman mosaic from North Africa.
"For he was naked"

Draught? In the first part of the story, seven people set out to fish in one boat; this is too large a crew for one boat, but ample for two. And if we note that the list of fishermen includes both Peter and the sons of Zebedee, it appears certain that on this occasion the two boats of the two families participated. And in fact, at the end of this fishing operation a second boat is mentioned, distinguished from the first by its size as a "small" boat in the Greek text. All of these elements fit very well the technique of operating the veranda nets.

The difficult part of the story comes at the end: "Jesus said to them, 'Bring some of the fish that you have just caught.' So Simon Peter went aboard and hauled the net ashore, full of large fish, a hundred and fifty-three of them; and although there were so many, the net was not torn. Jesus said to them, 'Come and have breakfast'. Now none of the disciple dared ask him, 'Who are you?' They knew it was the Lord. Jesus came and took the bread and gave it to them, and so with the fish." (John 21:10-13).

What is being said here? The fishermen meet Jesus after hauling their nets, but before releasing the entangled fish, a time-consuming process. They find that a meal has been prepared - as usual, bread and grilled fish. Here the story could have ended, but a new tale starts. Jesus asks Simon to bring the fish he had caught. Simon obeys, but instead of bringing fish from the full load in the boats, he hauls a new net up to the shore. It is clear that the reference is not to the nets already in the boat. This new net that Simon hauls alone could be only a cast-net, which as we known can be cast and hauled in by just one man. A seine, it must be repeated here, requires a crew for its operation; furthermore, this is impossible on the rocky shore of Tabgha.

What is more, a catch of 153 large fish - musht, of course, because no other fish could be caught in this time and place - in a cast-net would in itself be a miracle. But of course, this would be a minor miracle compared to the exploit of the two fully loaded boats. It appears that John added another tale, not mentioned in the other Gospels - the tale of a miraculous catch with a cast-net. Luke combined, as we know, two events: the miraculous catch and the calling of the brothers. John combined three events, two of which, however, are not compatible. Toward the end of John's account, Jesus confers the primacy on Peter by saying, "Feed my lambs", "Tend my sheep" (John 21:15).

Christian tradition ascribes the meeting place of Jesus with his disciples to the rock at the warm springs of Tabgha. From a fisherman's viewpoint, this is the correct choice. This is the area where musht schools

Interior of Church of the Primacy showing Mensa Domini, the stone table where the meal of fish and bread was eaten (picture of church appears on p. 29)

formerly concentrated in the winter. Here, too, Jesus met his disciples for the first time. On this rock, now known as the rock of the primacy of Peter, stands a small modern Franciscan chapel, "The Church of the Primacy of Peter". It was built on the foundations of earlier churches, the oldest dating from the first half of the fourth century. The altar is built around the stone outcroping, known to pilgrims as the Lord's Table (Mensa Domini), on which the fish meal was served.

Hook and Line and Saint Peter's Fish

Angling is mentioned only once in the Gospels, and then not in connection with ordinary fishing but as an enacted parable, or symbolic action. In early spring, the Hebrew month of Adar, Jesus met with his disciples for the last time in Capernaum: at this time, every adult Jewish male was required to pay a half-shekel tax to the Temple in Jerusalem. This gave the Pharisees an opportunity to test the loyalty of the strange preacher and his followers. Jesus did not approve of this Temple tax, but he did not yet wish his view to be widely known. According to the Gospels, Jesus avoids a clear answer.

"When they came to Caper'na-um, the collectors of the half-shekel tax went up to Peter and said, 'Does not your teacher pay the tax?' He said, 'Yes.' And when he came home, Jesus spoke to him first, saying, 'What do you think, Simon? From whom do kings of the earth take toll or tribute? From their sons or from others?'

"And when he said, 'From others,' Jesus said to him, 'Then the sons are free. However, not to give offense to them, go to the sea and cast a hook, and take the first fish that comes up, and when you open its mouth you will find a shekel; take that and give it to them for me and yourself." (Matt. 17:24-27).

It is because of this miracle that the musht was given the name "St Peter's Fish". However, from the realistic point of view - and in contradiction to all accepted tradition - it cannot have been the fish caught by

Sixth century mosaic from church in Hirbet Bet-Loya (Negev)
showing fisherman (Peter?) "casting a hook".
(Courtesy of Israel dept. of Antiquities and Museums)

Church mosaic,
Transjordan, sixth century

Peter with hook and line in this famous miracle. The reason is simple: the musht feeds on plankton and is not attracted by other food. It is therefore caught with nets, as we have already seen, and not with hook and line. The fishermen on the lake have, since time immemorial, used hook and line with sardine as bait to fish both barbels, which are predators and "bottom feeders", that is, they collect their food from the bottom of the lake. According to the distribution of fishing rights attributed to Joshua bin Nun as mentioned earlier, angling in the Lake was free and open to all tribes.

There can be only one explanation for the confusing change of name. It was good for tourism! The Sea of Galilee has always attracted visitors and pilgrims, and the musht is part of the unique local cuisine (today raised mostly in ponds). It is flat, and has practically no bones except for the spine, which is easily removed, is delicious when freshly fried. Long ago, just as today, it was possible to see fishing boats delivering their

Ancient fishermen catching barbels with hook and line.
Left: Egyptian; right: Assyrian

St Peter's fish waiting to be fried!

St Peter's fish served at the fish restaurant of Ein Gev

Kinneret Sailing boat entering Ein Gev harbour

catch to the eating places on the shore. In fact, the proverbial measure for speed, "as from the sea into the frying pan" appears in the Talmud as a metaphor for fast action, and was part of daily speech in Tiberias. This clearly refers to musht and not barbels, which are best when boiled.

The first Christians were local people and therefore familiar with the various fishing methods. They of course knew that the fish caught by Peter could only have been a barbel and not a musht. However, as pilgrims began to come from distant regions, it must have seemed good for business to give the name "St Peter's Fish" to the musht being served by the early lakeside eating houses. The most popular and easily prepared fish acquired the most marketable name!

In spite of this evidence, it is suggested in some circles that Simon Peter may nevertheless have caught a musht because of the practice of angling with a triple or quadruple hook. The fisherman (not the good fisherman) throws a line with a multiple hook into a school of fish and jerks the line sharply so that the hook enters the body of the fish. As a result, more fish are injured than caught and diseases may result. It is hard to imagine that the professional Jewish fishermen of Capernaum were guilty of such poor techniques. Today such practice is forbidden by law.

But even if, in this case, Saint Peter did not catch the fish in question, he still deserves to have his name associated with the best fish in the lake.

The "Small Fishes"

The Talmud mentions the names of about 50 fish, most of them of Greek or Aramaic origin, and a few of Hebrew. Only two of these names - Binit (barbels) and Tarit (sardines) - were and still are part of fishermen's talk at the Sea of Galilee. Adam gave names only to animals and birds. Biblical laws distinguishes between clean fish, those which Jews are permitted to eat (vertebrate) and unclean (without bones). Clean fish are generally recognized by the presence of fins and scales.

The reason for this "neglect" of detailed consideration of fish in the Old Testament is simple: The Old Testament experience was born in the desert, and fish were far less known than other living creatures. Nor were the writers of the Gospels much more familiar with the names of the fish of the lake; not knowing otherwise, they too classified them by general features. Thus, as we have noted in Matthew (13:48), the "bad" fish were the catfish (without scales - bad because these Jewish fishermen were still observant of the Mosaic laws of cleanliness) and the "good" were all the others in the catch. The Gospels mention another difference, that of size: the "large fish" - musht and barbel - and the "small", sardines. To prevent any error, John emphasises the size of 153 fish that Simon Peter brings upon the cast-net, calling them "big fish", because sardines can also be caught by the same method, but with a small-meshed net.

Sardine fishermen with gill nets, 1975

49

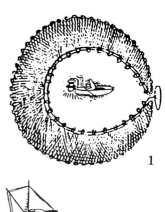

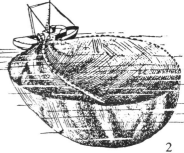

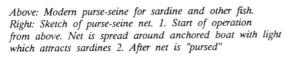

Above: Modern purse-seine for sardine and other fish.
Right: Sketch of purse-seine net. 1. Start of operation
from above. Net is spread around anchored boat with light
which attracts sardines 2. After net is "pursed"

Ein Gev fishermen unloading the sardine catch

In the Gospels, the "small fish" are mentioned clearly in the miracle of the feeding of the 4000. In Matthew (15:34) and Mark (8:7), which are the only versions that deal with this miracle, "seven loaves and a few small fish" are what the followers had brought to eat and from which the miracle grew.

The miracle of the feeding of the 5000 appears in all four Gospels. In Matthew (14:17), Mark (6:4) and Luke (9:13) the miracle grew out of "five loaves and two fish". John's version is different, and the Greek "opsarion" is used to describe the fish. The entire passage appears as follows in the King James version: "There is a lad here, which hath five barley loaves and two small fishes, but what are they among so many?" (John 6:9).

We may assume from both versions that the small fish were not young individuals of large species, but sardines which are by nature small. These, with bread, in fact made up the staple diet of the local population. This assumption is supported by the first century Roman writer Strabo, who wrote that the Sea of Galilee provided the fish best suited for salting. The center of the salting industry was the town of Magdala, called in Greek Tarichaea (meaning place where fish are salted). Which fish are most suited for this industry? Obviously not the large fish, for which, sold fresh, there was always a good market with the local population. By comparison, the sardines, which appear in large quantities and during a short season, had to be preserved by salting. It is the salted sardine which the Talmud refers to as "Tarit".

Sardine fisherman throwing cast-net. Right: sketch showing retrieving apparatus

The mosaic at the Church of the Multiplication

The two small fish are pictured in a mosaic at Tabgha, in the Church of the Multiplication, which was built to commemorate the miracle. We see a basket with four loaves, and the fish on either side. But now another problem faces us! These fish do not appear to be from our lake at all! All fish caught in the Kinneret have only a single dorsal fin, while those shown in the mosaic have two dorsal fins. This must mean that the artist who designed the Tabgha mosaic and who almost certainly came from abroad to do the job, worked, as all artists did, from a prepared pattern; he clearly did not make it his business to inspect the fish in the Kinneret.

Storms

Storms appear in the Gospels on two occasions. In one, the disciples are returning before nightfall from the miraculous feeding, and Jesus bids them to go back: "Immediately he made his disciples get into the boat and go before him to the other side, to Beth-sa'ida, while he dismissed the crowd. And after he had taken leave of them, he went up on the mountain to pray. And when evening came, the boat was out on the sea, and he was alone on the land. And he saw that they were making headway painfully, for the wind was against them. And about the fourth watch of the night he came to them, walking on the sea. He meant to pass by them, but when they saw him walking on the sea they thought it was a ghost, and cried out; for they all saw him, and were terrified. But immediately he spoke to them and said, 'Take heart, it is I; have no fear.' And he got into the boat with them and the wind ceased." (Mark 6:45-51).

52

An easterly storm on the Sea of Galilee

53

Matthew and John give similar descriptions, but Matthew adds another maritime event - Peter's unsuccessful attempt to walk upon the waters too!

"Lord, if it is you, bid me come to you on the water. He said, 'Come.' So Peter got out of the boat and walked on the water and came to Jesus; but when he saw the wind, he was afraid, and beginning to sink he cried out, 'Lord, save me.' Jesus immediately reached out his hand and caught him, saying to him, 'O man of little faith, why did you doubt?" (Matt. 14:28-31).

The location of the miraculous feeding is generally put at the north-eastern part of the lake, near Bethsaida. According to Mark and Matthew, after this stormy voyage the ship finally reaches the western shore (Land of Gennesaret). But according to John it reaches Capernaum, which was their destination, in safety. Both cases indicate the ship heading into a winter storm, either southerly or westerly.

The other stormy event occurs when Jesus, again on a winter evening, sails with his disciples from Capernaum to Kursi. "One day he got into a boat with his disciples, and he said to them, 'Let us go across to the other side of the lake.' So they set out and as they sailed he fell asleep. And a storm of wind came down on the lake, and they were filling with water, and were in danger. And they went and woke him, saying, 'Master, Master, we are perishing!' And he awoke and rebuked the wind and the raging waves; and they ceased, and there was a calm. He said to them, 'Where is your faith?' And they were afraid, and they marveled, saying to one another, 'Who then is this, that he commands even wind and water, and they obey him?" (Luke 8:22-25. Parallel accounts are in Matthew 8:23-27; Mark 4:35-41).

This is an accurate and detailed description of an eastern storm on the Kinneret. It fits precisely the tales of contemporary fishermen who have sailed to fish for sardines at Kursi and were caught in transit by the well-known eastern storm, called "Sharkia" in Arabic ("shark", as we know, means east in Arabic). Even today this storm, which usually starts in the early evening, is good cause for apprehension among fishermen.

Weather Forecasts

Gazing at the skies to forecast the weather is an age-old custom the world over. It was done, as well, by the ancient residents of the Kinneret, since knowing the moods of the lake was essential for their activities. We find an echo of this in Jesus' sayings:

"And the Pharisees and Sad'ducees came, and to test him they asked him

A westerly storm at Ein Gev harbour

Sennabris harbour: a calm day

*Breakwater of ancient harbour of Hippos, on eastern shore,
one of "the coasts of Decapolis" (Mark 7,31)*

*Ancient harbour of Gergesa where the boat of Jesus and his disciples
landed. At right, behind the grove of trees, the traditional precipice
from which the swine rushed to the sea*

to show them a sign from heaven. He answered them, 'When it is evening, you say, "It will be fair weather; for the sky is red." And in the morning, "It will be stormy today, for the sky is red and threatening." You know how to interpret the appearance of the sky, but you cannot interpret the signs of the times." (Matt. 16:1-3).

And indeed, natural phenomena have not changed in our region: a red evening sky means fair weather around the lake the following day, and for most of the country as well. (In fact, this holds true for other parts of the world, as the old sailor's ditty tells us: "Red sky at night, sailors' delight.")

This has, of course, a scientific explanation. A red sunset indicates a stable atmosphere; because there are no upward air currents, dust in the atmosphere remains close to the earth and these particles refract rays of light into red. This is also true for the morning forecast: the atmosphere is stable, but the appearance of low clouds signifies a possible change from fair weather to rainy. ("Red skies in the morning, sailors take warning!")

This weather forecast as it appears in Matthew is accurate, and confirmed by generations of Kinneret residents, including this writer. On the other hand, Luke's version is different both in content and credibility: "He also said to the multitudes, 'When you see a cloud rising in the west, you say at once, "A shower is coming;" and so it happens. And when you see the south wind blowing, you say, "There will be scorching heat"; and it happens. You hypocrites! You know how to interpret the appearance of earth and sky; but why do you not know how to interpret the present time?" (Luke 12:54-56).

The first part of this forecast, with rain clouds coming from the west, is generally true for all the country. The second part, however, does not fit the Kinneret region. It does hold true for the southern part of Israel, where the winds from the south, coming from the hot and dry Negev region, bring warm days during spring and autumn.

The differences in the two versions should not surprise the reader. Luke was acquainted with Jerusalem and Judaea, but was unfamiliar with the geography and climate of Galilee. And so he attributes to Jesus a weather prediction that applies to the meteorology of Jerusalem.

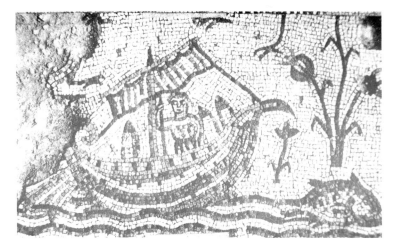

Fifth century mosaic, Beit Shean

Summary

Having dealt with this collection of biblical excerpts about fishing and natural phenomena of the Sea of Galilee, we see that the parables and stories of the Gospels have unique historical value. This is in spite of the many stylistic changes which the original texts have undergone for theological or other reasons.

Suddenly, a hitherto unknown world is revealed to us, one not to be found in any other sources. This is a world of Jewish fishermen, living and working on the Sea of Galilee during the crucial period toward the end of the Second Temple. The picture that emerges is true, rich in its simplicity, dynamic, and centered on a search for answers to life's basic question.

Roman coin of Tiberias

First century mosaic, Magdala

The details of the picture are many and diverse. We have glimpsed a variety of intimate scenes: fishermen's families passing from father to son; owners of fishing boats and other fishing gear; employers working with hired help for rowing and hauling ropes and nets; co-operation among boats in the limited fishing area at Tabgha near Capernaum; co-ordination of boats and nets in pursuit of the wily musht by day with the help of an observer on shore; night work with the trammel nets, followed by washing them the morning after; the diving of the naked cast-net fisherman into the cold winter waters; the quickly changing fortunes of the fisherman, that can shift from bad luck at night to overloaded boats in the morning; hook and line cast to catch barbel; sorting the seine catch to keep the clean and throw out the unclean fish; breakfast of bread and grilled fish after the night's toil; Jesus's followers with their bundles of bread and pickled sardines, as their master says, "Or what man of you, if his son asks him for bread, will give him a stone? Or if he asks for a fish, will give him a serpent?" (Matt. 7:9-10).

And even these two references of stone and serpent are taken from the fisherman's daily experience. They symbolize the frustration of a disappointing catch, for it often happens that instead of fish the net brings in mostly stones, and it may even occur that together with the fish the haul may bring up the water serpent, which is common in the lake.

We have also seen the red sunset and the threatening sunrise. And we have almost heard (as this writer so often has) the howling of the storm as the fishermen toil to advance in the face of the angry waves.

Roman coins of Tiberias with maritime motifs

And finally, we must note here the punishment meted out to sinners: "Whoever causes one of these little ones who believes in me to sin, it would be better for him if a great millstone were hung round his neck and he were thrown into the sea" (Mark 9:42).

These vignettes give another dimension to the special affection felt by Christians everywhere for the Sea of Galilee.

And here is the place to recall why the fish became the secret sign of the new faith when it was the persecuted brotherhood. In the catacombs of Rome, where early Christians gathered to pray in secret, pictures of fish were discovered, painted and carved into the walls. There is also a second, and apparently later, explanation for the fish as symbol of Christianity. The first letters of the Greek words "Jesous Christos, theou hyios soter" (Jesus Christ, son of God and Saviour) form the acronym "Ichthys", which means fish in Greek.

Finally, let us not forget that Jesus and his disciples, the fishermen of the Sea of Galilee, were loyal Jews living in accordance with their religious laws, who at a time of great historical crisis followed a new leader to bring about redemption.

It was only after the heroes of the gospels were long dead that Christianity began to evolve in different forms.

Boat in the Dead Sea, 6th century mosaic in church of Madaba, Transjordan

Town square of Magdala, first century,
excavated by Franciscan Institute in the 1970's

Ancient harbour of Magdala. The boat was discovered behind
the breakwater, upper left

The boat from Magdala

The discovery of an ancient boat from the time of Jesus, well preserved in the mud near Madgala, created great excitement throughout the world early in 1986. The boat was unquestionably in use for both fishing and transportation for many years during the first century C.E. - a time that was crucial for the history of the Jews, and for the entire world. The discovery was made by two brothers, fishermen from nearby Kibbutz Ginossar.

The boat, now in a specially constructed preservation pool at Beit Yigal Allon at Kibbutz Ginnosar, is 9 meters long, 2.5 meters wide, and 1.25 meters high. As we know, these are almost exactly the measurements of the boats used by the seine net fishermen.

How did this boat, made of wooden planks from the cedars of Lebanon, with ribs of oak branches, survive for nearly 2000 years? It was apparently left at a dockyard when no longer in use, and partially dismantled. During this process, the boat was covered with silt carried down by flooding from a nearby stream. It was this "packaging" of mud that preserved the boat so miraculously.

It has been called the Kinneret Boat, the Magdala Boat, the Galilee Boat, and the Jesus Boat, and it is the first actual and detailed message from the maritime and fishing history of the Kinneret which we have received from the past.

Discovery of the boat, January 1986

Excavation of the boat, February 1986

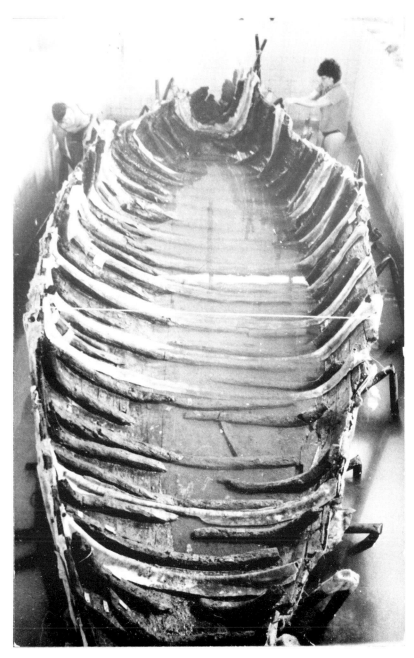

The boat in the conservation pool (Photo: Danny Friedman)

Bibliography

Gustaf Dalman: *Arbeit und Sitte in Palästina,* Band 6 Gutersloh 1939.

Gustaf Dalman: *Sacred Sites and Ways,* London 1935.

James Hornell: *Fishing in Many Waters,* Cambridge 1950.

James Hornell: *Report of the Fisheries of Palestine,* London 1935.

Rudolf de Haas: *"Galilee, the Sacred Sea",* Jerusalem 1933.

E. Masterman: *Studies in Galilee,* Chicago 1909.

Moritz Mainzer: *Ueber Jagd Fischfang und Bienenzucht bei den Juden in der Tannaeischen Zeit,* Frankfurt am Main 1910.

Samuel Krauss, *Talmudische Archäologie,* Frankfurt am Main 1910-1912.

P. Franz Dunkel: Die Fischerei am See Genesareth und das Neue Testament, *Biblica 1924.*

Mendel Nun: *Ancient Jewish Fisheries* (Hebrew), Tel-Aviv 1964, 232 p.

Printed by Ariel Publishing House, Jerusalem